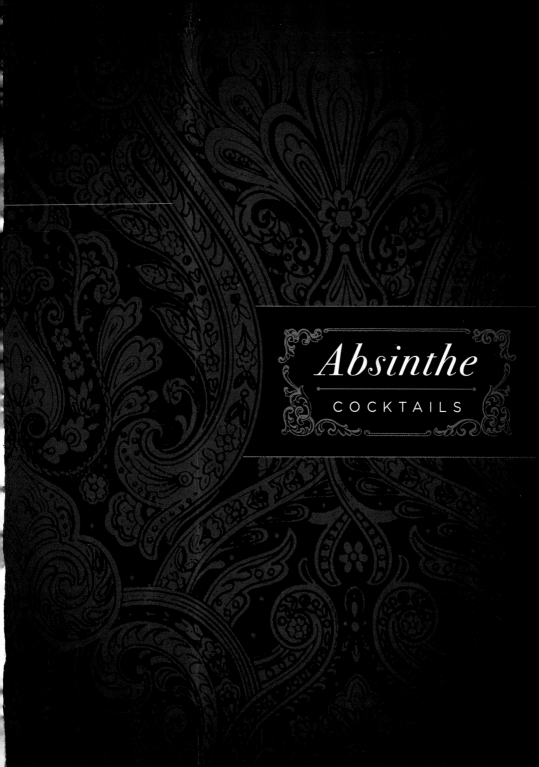

Absinthe

COCKTAILS

Absinthe

COCKTAILS

50 Ways
to Mix with the
GREEN FAIRY

BY KATE SIMON

PHOTOGRAPHS BY
LARA FERRONI

CHRONICLE BOOKS
SAN FRANCISCO

Library of Congress Cataloging-in-Publication
Data available.

ISBN 978-0-8118-7329-1

Manufactured in China

Design and typesetting by Gregory Ryan Klein
Food and prop styling by Lara Ferroni
The photographer wishes to thank Lorna Yee
for her help in styling and Gwydion Stone for
the generous use of his absinthe fountain and
glassware. A portion of the product pictured in
the photographs was provided by The Thomas
Collective and Pernod Ricard USA.

Angostura Bitters is a registered trademark
of Angostura Ltd. Bénédictine is a registered
trademark of B and B Liqueur. Bittermens'
Xocolatl Mole Bitters is a registered trademark
of Bittermens, Inc. Cherry Heering is a registered
trademark of Peter F. Heering. Clément Créole
Shrubb is a registered trademark of Clement USA.
Inc. Peychaud's is a registered trademark of
The Sazerac Company, Inc.

10 9 8 7 6 5 4 3 2 1

Chronicle Books LLC
680 Second Street
San Francisco, California 94107
www.chroniclebooks.com

TABLE of CONTENTS

Acknowledgments

I had the pleasure of working with so many absinthe-minded people on this book; it was a group effort. Immense thanks to Gwydion Stone for his guidance and support. Thanks also to Ted Breaux, not only for sharing his knowledge with me but for kindly reintroducing absinthe to a thirsty public. Others who helped make this book a reality include Erik Adkins, B. Alex, Eric Alperin, Faye Bender, Marc Bernhard, Jeff Berry, Greg Best, Sarah Billingsley, Chris Bostick, Jamie Boudreau, Lu Brow, Jackson Cannon, Laura Cassidy, Santino Cicciari, Anne Donnard, Lucy Farber, Lara Ferroni, Ted Haigh, Chris Hannah, David Hawk, Sarah Hearn, Christian Hodgkinson, Jeff Hollinger, Amber Holst, Daniel Hyatt, Charles Joly, Misty Kalkofen, Ben Kasman, Gregory Ryan Klein, Ravi Lalchandani, Bill LeBlond, Scott Leopold, Brian MacGregor, Toby Maloney, Jim Meehan, Brian Miller, Kamal Mukherjee, Doug Ogan, Ales Olasz, Peter Perez, Julie Reiner, Jim Romdall, Mark Rutherford, Peter Schaf, Riccardo Semeria, Dave Shenaut, Daniel Shoemaker, Allie Smith, LeNell Smothers, Marcos Tello, Jerusha Torres, Charles Vexenat, Thad Vogler, Phil Ward, Alyssa Winters, Evan Zimmerman, and the members of the online communities at the Wormwood Society, the Virtual Absinthe Museum, and La Fée Verte, whose message board discussions and product reviews proved both enlightening and entertaining. Cheers to the late cocktailians and distillers who left a legacy of delicious drinks, and to the booze historians who have kept the recipes alive.

Introduction

Mention absinthe, and people do funny things with their eyebrows. When I confessed that I was compiling a book of absinthe cocktails, most people responded with one of three facial expressions. Most common was the skeptical, single-brow raise: "You make cocktails with that stuff? Isn't it illegal? Isn't it a hallucinogen that will, like, make you go crazy?" The more adventurous, but still misguided, would raise both brows enthusiastically and then invite themselves over for research: "Absinthe, huh? The green fairy! My buddy brought a bottle back from Amsterdam one time . . . that stuff is *insane*! Do you light the cocktails on fire?" Then there was the furrowed brow, and the wince: "Oooh, never again. I tried absinthe once. It tasted like licorice-flavored cough syrup. I don't know how people drink that stuff."

Poor absinthe. It's a victim of its own shoddy publicity. Starting in the 1990s, companies selling fake absinthe on the Web created a whole lot of hype about the spirit, most of it humorously false. They were recycling the bogus, politically charged claims that got absinthe outlawed in the United States and other countries eighty years earlier. Even worse, the hideous, bright green booze they were selling wasn't absinthe at all. Scammers would mix cheap grain spirits with food coloring and artificial flavors and charge $100 a bottle, promising hallucinogenic, aphrodisiacal, Ecstasy-like effects. They would even invent bizarre rituals, like lighting sugar cubes on fire. The fact that absinthe was banned in the United States and other countries, and that very few people knew anything about the true absinthe of old, was a boon to these swindlers—it bred intrigue.

But things are changing. Authentic absinthe is now available legally. And when I tell people about this book, there's a fourth group that responds with a more welcome facial expression: a look of recognition. Increasingly, people are tasting true absinthe and learning that just like any other premium spirit, it's not a hallucinogen, and when it's served the proper way, it's no stronger than a glass of wine. It's only slightly sweet—due to the naturally sweet herbs anise and fennel—and slightly bitter. True to its reputation, absinthe does have flavor characteristics similar to black licorice, among other herbal notes.

Absinthe was a standard cocktail ingredient from the late nineteenth century into the 1920s. It lent depth and a whisper of anise to mixed drinks. By 1915, absinthe had been banned in the United States, France, and several other countries, but it continued to enhance cocktails at London's Savoy Hotel and bars in Cuba and Spain, where it remained legal. Eventually, with absinthe outlawed in several key countries and production slashed, bartenders turned to a new crop of anise-flavored substitutes, known as pastis. Pastis is sweeter than absinthe and less complex, notably lacking the herb wormwood, which lends absinthe a unique bitter element. Gradually the classic absinthe cocktails—now made with the less dynamic pastis—fell out of favor. By the 1960s, cocktail culture was fizzling out altogether, trumped by beer and colorful, two-ingredient vodka drinks.

In recent years, cocktails have made an impressive comeback, but absinthe, still unavailable, was left out of the mix until 2007, when it made its long-awaited reprise. Classic cocktails like the rye whiskey–based Sazerac (page 33) and the herbaceous Chrysanthemum (page 35) are back. And the influx of authentic European absinthe and artisanal domestic brands has inspired a new wave of absinthe-laced cocktails like the rum-based Stargazer (page 61), the elegant Gill Sans (page 69), and the flirtatious L'amour en Fuite (page 95).

Cocktail hour has merged with *l'heure verte*, the storied "green hour" of the Belle Époque. Absinthe, the green fairy, the emerald muse, is painting our cocktails in shades of pale, opalescent green. The myths have been exposed, and some of the mystique has faded, but the romance remains. Dust off the vintage glassware—it's time to drink to history.

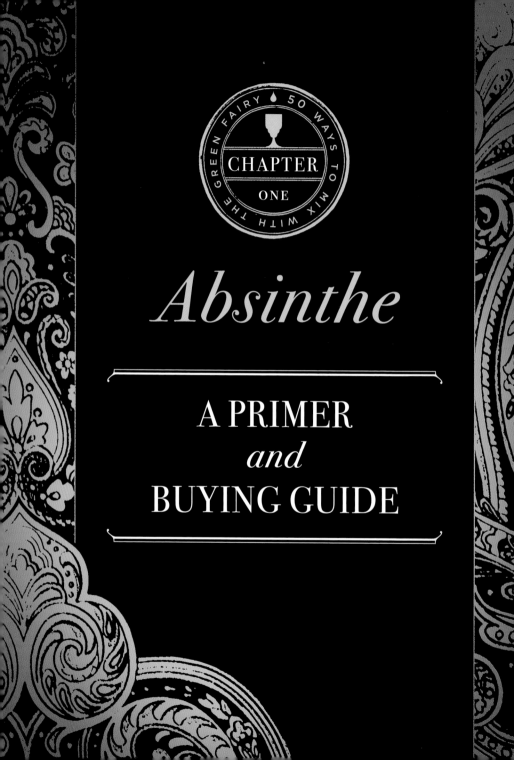

CHAPTER
ONE

50 WAYS TO MIX WITH THE GREEN FAIRY

Absinthe

A PRIMER *and* BUYING GUIDE

Absinthe is a distilled spirit made with a variety of herbs, defined by its anise-forward flavor and its slightly bitter wormwood note. Its character is herbal and slightly sweet. Most absinthe is pale green in color, its pigment derived from herbs, but some absinthe is colorless. And still others are colored artificially. (For a full description of the three types of absinthe, see the Absinthe Buying Guide later in this chapter.)

Absinthe is bottled at a high strength—60 to 68 percent alcohol by volume—and designed to be tempered with water and enjoyed as an aperitif or mixed into cocktails. (Learn how to prepare a traditional glass of absinthe on page 29.) When water is added, it reacts with the anise and fennel oils and the absinthe shows its *louche*, transforming into an opalescent, milky white color. It's a marvelous metamorphosis, and it's easy to see why this peculiar drink attracted such mystique in its time. It was like magic.

Absinthe was born in the eighteenth century in western Switzerland and was first produced on a large scale in eastern France, all of its early life centered near the Franco-Swiss border. Like many herbal spirits, it was conceived as a folk remedy—a tonic designed to cure a variety of ailments. It became known as *la fée verte*, the green fairy, and by the mid-nineteenth century, Europe was entranced. This green goddess was favored, famously, by French writers and painters, becoming notoriously linked to the Parisian artistic class. But its reach wasn't limited to artists. Absinthe flowed like wine during the decadent, high-living Belle Époque—beautiful era—that started in the 1890s and partied hard until the First World War. With French wine production devastated by widespread vineyard disease, and some absinthe brands available cheaply due to new methods of mass production and a switch to inferior ingredients, *la fée verte* reigned. It's said that in the 1890s, absinthe was served in as many as 30,000 cafés in Paris alone.

Bartenders took notice of this robust spirit. Just a dash of absinthe in a cocktail could deliver a vibrant bouquet of herbal flavors, at once bitter and sweet, and a bigger dose lent cocktails a savory wallop and an otherworldly opalescence. In 1930, bartender Harry Craddock listed more than 100 absinthe cocktails in his *Savoy Cocktail Book*, which chronicled the drinks served at London's Savoy Hotel in the glam '20s.

But the party was ending. Absinthe was all but dried up. By 1915, it had been banned in the United States, France, Switzerland, Holland, Belgium, and Brazil. It was deemed poisonous and blamed for widespread alcoholism, mental and physical illnesses, suicides, murders, and the general debauchery of the hard-drinking artistic set. (It was infamously pinned for making Van Gogh slice off part of his ear.)

Governments, teetotalers, and lobbyists for the struggling French wine industry pointed at wormwood, one of the key herbs used to make absinthe. In high doses, wormwood sent lab animals into convulsions. But recent research has let absinthe off the hook, it never contained dangerous amounts of thujone, the potentially harmful chemical compound present in wormwood. A common anecdote among contemporary absinthe enthusiasts is that if a person actually wanted to experience thujone-induced convulsions from drinking absinthe, he would have to drink so much that he would surely die of alcohol poisoning first.

Like any booze that's available on the cheap, absinthe was favored by binge drinkers, which didn't help its image. What's worse is that the cheapest brands were colored artificially with crude, dangerous chemicals. Researchers have since discovered that if people were getting sick and going crazy from absinthe, the culprit was probably these additives. But at the time, absinthe took the hit in the public's eye. Absinthe was burned at the stake and pronounced dead, but it was really just taking a ninety-year nap. (And, in fact, it lived on in Spain, where it continued to be produced legally to little fanfare, and in Switzerland, where moonshiners disguised the infamous green spirit by making it colorless.) In 2000, legal absinthe production resumed in France, and in 2005, Switzerland lifted its ban. Two years later, New Orleans–born chemist and absinthe historian Ted Breaux released Lucid in the United States—the first absinthe available legally in that country in almost a century. The word on the street was that the ban had been lifted, but, in fact, it remained in place. Rather, Breaux and his colleagues had found a loophole of sorts. The wording of the law, which had originally banned absinthe by name, had been modified and generalized over the years, eventually prohibiting any beverages or foods with more than 10 ppm of thujone, without specifying absinthe. Breaux and his colleagues tested vintage bottlings of pre-ban absinthe and found that they came in under the mark—they contained far less thujone than was previously thought. Premium contemporary absinthes, which are nearly identical to premium pre-ban absinthes, also contain only trace amounts of thujone. Turns out absinthe is as legal as turkey stuffing, which can also include trace amounts of thujone if it's made with the common ingredient sage.

The green fairy is back, and the cocktail-prone are celebrating in the way they do best—with a dash here and a few generous drops there. Absinthe has been reunited with its old mates rye whiskey, brandy, gin, rum, vermouth, violet liqueur, and Bénédictine. And it's made some new friends, like premium tequila, fresh strawberries, and liqueurs of elderflower and ginger. This book is filled with fantastic recipes—both classic and contemporary cocktails—from some of the best bartenders in the craft, representing the top bars in the United States and Europe. Before you start mixing, here's a guide to buying authentic absinthe, and tips on getting a taste for the emerald muse without spending too much green.

ABSINTHE BUYING GUIDE

There are two types of premium absinthe: *verte* (green) and *blanche* (colorless). Most fall into the first category, possessing a natural pale green hue, but there are good examples of the blanche category, too. There's a third category, usually inferior in quality, which is not distilled with herbs but rather mixed with herbal oils before bottling (see Compounded Absinthe, page 18).

This guide reflects the brands available in the United States at the time of this writing. The contemporary absinthe category is growing fast, so some of these brands may change or cease production, and certainly new brands will become available. You can keep up to date by visiting the Web sites listed in the Resources section in the back of this book, or by talking with your favorite local spirits purveyor or bartender.

VERTE

This is absinthe in its most classic form. In the best examples, a base spirit derived from grapes, grain, or beets is infused and distilled with herbs, including green anise, wormwood, fennel, and other botanicals like hyssop and melissa. It's then infused again with more herbs, picking up additional flavors and aromas as well as its pale green color. These absinthes are dynamic and multi-dimensional, blooming on the palate with a bright, sweet burst of anise and other herbs, anchored by a spine of peppery, tannic wormwood.

There are several excellent artisanal brands made domestically, which are good for sipping in the traditional manner or mixing in cocktails. Delaware Phoenix (upstate New

York) makes two delicate absinthes, the floral, grassy Meadow of Love and the lush Walton Waters; Leopold Brothers (Denver) is sweet, spicy, and bright; Marteau (Portland, Oregon) is elegant and well-balanced, yet assertive, and performs well in cocktails; Pacifique (Seattle) is well-rounded and subtle, made according to a nineteenth-century French recipe; St. George (San Francisco) is deeply herbal with a hint of fruit; Sirène (Chicago) is crisp and complex, designed for cocktails; and Vieux Carré (Philadelphia) is soulful, spicy, and packaged in a handsome square bottle.

Good European-made brands with distribution channels in the United States include Duplais (Switzerland), a punchy offering with a bitter wormwood edge; Lucid (France), which led the U.S. absinthe revival, is mild in flavor, approachable, and widely available; Mansinthe (Switzerland), a lively formula created by gothcore musician Marilyn Manson; Nouvelle-Orléans (France), a light, floral tribute to New Orleans and its long love affair with absinthe; Obsello (Spain), a unique, bold-flavored absinthe, with rich, nutty characteristics and a supple body; and Vieux Pontarlier (France), a bright, grassy, classical absinthe made in a nineteenth-century distillery.

There are many coveted European absinthe brands that aren't regularly distributed in the United States but are obtainable online. For a list of Web sites that specialize in overseas absinthe, see the Resources section.

BLANCHE

Colorless absinthe was termed *la bleue* in post-ban Switzerland. It was moonshine, distilled secretly and circulated right under the noses of unsuspecting officials, who would have expected absinthe to be the usual green color. Premium offerings are distilled with the same herbs found in absinthe verte and bottled while the product is still clear, skipping the coloration step. Recommended brands include La Clandestine, a Swiss product based on an illicit 1935 recipe and produced in the village where absinthe is said to have originated; and Kübler, another Swiss product, which has been made by one family since 1863 and, at under $50 a bottle, is one of the better values in the absinthe category.

COMPOUNDED ABSINTHE

Also called "oil mixes," these products consist of a neutral base spirit that has been infused with essential oils or whole herbs, with no additional distillation. Though this method existed in absinthe's pre-ban heyday, it was—and is—usually inferior to distilled absinthe. Ideally, compounded absinthe would be made with high-quality, steam-distilled essential oils and colored naturally with herbs, but that's seldom the case. Unfortunately, even though oil mixes are cheaper and easier to make, they're not always priced lower than well-made absinthe—some bottles cost $75 or more. Be wary of these products, as they often claim to be premium or extra-special in some way and rarely advertise the fact that they're not distilled. If a label says something like "neutral base spirit with natural flavors added" or lists artificial colors, check with a trusted source before you spend money on a bottle. Some experts believe it's possible to make a compounded absinthe that's better than decent, and at the time of this writing at least one producer is fixing to do so. For now, the most notable example is Pernod Absinthe, which is omnipresent in cocktail bars around the world but is colored artificially and is not as complex or assertive as most herb-distilled absinthes.

HOW TO GO GREEN
WITHOUT GOING
BROKE

At $40 to $90 a bottle, absinthe prices can be hard to swallow. Consider, however, that absinthe is no more expensive than premium tequila or scotch and that, because it's traditionally diluted with four or five parts water in the glass, or added to cocktails in mere dashes, a bottle can last a long time. Even so, there are ways to maximize the money you spend on absinthe. One is to shop wisely, to make sure you're buying a quality product and not wasting your precious cash on fancy packaging. With absinthe, price does not necessarily indicate quality. There are some good absinthes available for $50 or less and some inferior brands that are priced considerably higher. A little research can save you a lot of money. Take note of the recommendations in this book, read product reviews online (see a list of good sites in the Resources section of this book), join an absinthe forum, or talk to a knowledgeable bartender or spirits seller before you buy. Another way to save is to go in on a bottle with a group of friends and get together to celebrate *l'heure verte*. This way everyone gets a taste for a fraction of the cost of a bottle. Do this once a month and before long you'll be an expert. Cocktails are another great way to maximize your enjoyment of a bottle of absinthe. Many of the recipes in this book call for only a few drops or a fraction of an ounce of absinthe—a little goes a long way. You could work your way through all fifty recipes with a single bottle of absinthe.

CHAPTER

TWO

Before you pour

HOW to APPROACH
the recipes
IN THIS BOOK

BRANDS
AND SUBSTITUTIONS

Many of the cocktails in this book specify a particular absinthe. This reflects the specific flavor profile the recipe's creator was going for, given the products that were available to him or her. You can substitute another well-made absinthe. When making substitutions, be prepared to adjust proportions of other ingredients if warranted by the new flavor profile.

Beyond absinthe, some of the cocktails in this book call for other spirits by brand name. Again, the requested brands reflect the specific flavor profile that the creator was going for. In all cases, you can substitute other brands. Keep in mind that quality does matter even in mixed drinks—for the best results, choose high-quality ingredients. That doesn't mean you should take out a loan to stock your liquor cabinet. There are some well-made mid-shelf spirits that have managed to keep relatively low prices. Just research your purchases before you buy to make sure you're getting the most quality for your money.

Stocking up on spirits and other cocktail ingredients can be expensive, but as long as you're drinking responsibly—please do—each bottle should go a long way. One method for keeping costs down is to shop for just one cocktail at a time. Pick a cocktail, gather the ingredients, and, when you're ready to try another one, browse the book for a recipe that calls for some of the same spirits as the first, so you don't have to buy a whole new set of ingredients.

MEASURING ABSINTHE

Because the cocktails in this book are meant to showcase absinthe, it might seem peculiar that many of them call for only a few drops or a fraction of a teaspoon of absinthe. Resist the urge to blindly add more before you've tasted the cocktail. Because premium absinthe can be robust and flavorful, you might be surprised what a few drops can do. Many bartenders treat absinthe like bitters, measuring one drop at a time with an eye dropper. Small glass bottles with droppers can be purchased online or at herb-supply stores. You can also repurpose old dropper bottles that once held essential oils or medicines—just be sure to wash them well first to get rid of any die-hard scents.

BITTERS

The bitters category has swelled with new products in recent years. In addition to old-fashioned aromatic bitters, like the ubiquitous Angostura, there are bitters with dominating notes of celery, mint, and even chocolate. Bitters are to cocktails what salt and spices are to food. Feel free to spice your cocktails to taste and to experiment with different bitters brands or flavors. But do so with a light hand; sometimes the difference between one dash and two is a ruined cocktail.

SWEETENERS

The most common sweetener used in this book is simple syrup, a solution of equal parts sugar and water. You can use any type of crystallized sugar, but darker, less refined sugars yield a richer syrup. Try Demerara or turbinado sugar (the widely available Sugar in the Raw brand is an example of the latter) or others made from pure dehydrated or evaporated cane juice. To make simple syrup, combine one part sugar and one part water in a saucepan over low heat, stirring frequently until the sugar is dissolved. Remove from the heat and let cool to room temperature. Pour the syrup into a glass bottle with a stopper and store it in the refrigerator. It should keep well for up to two weeks. To prolong the shelf life, add half an ounce of vodka for every cup of syrup.

It's easy to create flavored syrups by adding herbs, fruit, nuts, or spices to simple syrup. Grenadine, a pomegranate-flavored syrup, is used in some recipes in this book. You can buy grenadine at spirits shops and many grocery stores, but homemade grenadine is a real treat. See the recipe on page 36.

Honey and agave nectar are two celebrated sweeteners that can be used in cocktails that call for simple syrup. Create a pourable syrup by thinning the viscous sweeteners with water (see the recipe for agave syrup on page 55). Note that honey and agave have distinct flavor profiles and, if used in place of simple syrup, can change a cocktail dramatically. Both are sweeter than table sugar and should be used in smaller amounts.

ADJUSTING FOR TASTE

Every palate is different, and your taste buds may prefer a cocktail a little sweeter, or with a bit less of this or that, than what was intended. When experimenting with proportions, it's a good idea to be conservative—start with small doses and add more to taste.

CITRUS PEEL GARNISHES

Garnishes are not just decoration—they complement a cocktail's flavors and help tie the whole drink together. In this book, and in the cocktail world at large, the most common garnishes are citrus peels. Fresh lemons, limes, oranges, and grapefruits hold sweet and tangy flavor-packed oils in their skins. The idea is to manually extract the oil by squeezing or twisting a swath of peel over the surface of a cocktail. After distributing the oils into the drink in this way, you may discard the used peel or drop it into the glass for further flavoring and decoration. Most recipes specify which action to take, but, in practice, it's always a matter of personal preference.

You can make citrus peel garnishes with a channel knife if you prefer a long thin strip; a wider garnish knife or citrus peeler if you're going for a wider ribbon of peel; or a standard bar knife to cut a swath of peel to your desired shape. For the latter free-cut method, first lay a whole, washed, uncut citrus fruit on a cutting board. Slice off both ends, then hollow out the fruit with a serrated knife and a spoon, saving the flesh for juicing or another purpose, leaving only the shell. Make a lateral cut through the peel, from one open end to the other, then flatten it, skin-side down, on a cutting board. Use a knife to scrape off any remaining bits of bitter pith. Cut the peel into strips, squares, or decorative shapes. A swath two inches in length and half an inch wide is usually sufficient, but you can cut larger pieces for dramatic effect. For the juiciest peels, choose the freshest citrus you can find, with plump, shiny skin. Store at room temperature and use within a week.

GLASSWARE

Because absinthe has so much history, it's fun to use old-timey glassware. Lovely vintage cocktail glasses are surprisingly easy to find at thrift stores, estate sales, antiques shops, or, if you're lucky, your grandmother's china cabinet. You might occasionally score a matching set, but it's also fun to collect distinctive pieces for an eclectic effect. In this book, when a recipe calls for a stemmed glass, a coupe or saucer glass is recommended, if only for the cool retro look (think Nick and Nora Charles). These are usually short with wide, shallow bowls and hold 3 to 6 ounces of liquid. Vintage specimens abound, and reproductions are making their way onto the shelves of the big kitchen retailers. In a pinch, any stemmed glass will do, from a wineglass to those V-shaped martini glasses that were so ubiquitous in recent decades.

Rocks glasses, also called tumblers, buckets, lowballs, or old-fashioneds, are stemless and sturdy. They're the go-to glasses for short drinks served over ice ("on the rocks") as well as bold Sazerac-style drinks that, despite being served neat (without ice), are decidedly too muscular for dainty stemmed glasses. Rocks-style glasses are usually available in two sizes: single (6 to 8 ounces) or double (10 to 12 ounces). Take your pick based on the volume of the drink and what feels good in your hand.

When a recipe calls for a tall glass, any tall, narrow vessel will do. They're sometimes sold as chimneys, highballs, or Collins glasses, and they generally hold between 10 and 16 ounces.

Some fizzes call for a juice glass—the kind that's at home on the breakfast table. These are similar in shape to a highball but slightly smaller, holding between 5 and 8 ounces. Ball and Kerr make 8-ounce jelly jars that work as farm table–chic alternatives.

ABSINTHE ACCOUTREMENTS

When preparing a traditional glass of absinthe (learn how on page 29), it's fun to have the right paraphernalia. Classic absinthe glasses—which were typically stemmed, with tapered bowls, and sometimes featured bulbous reservoirs that served as dosage guides—are obtainable at antiques shops and stores that specialize in vintage barware. As absinthe has regained popularity, reproductions of classic vessels have started to pop up in kitchen stores. Absinthe spoons were ornate, sometimes plated in silver, and were designed to serve as strainers, resting across the top of an absinthe glass, holding a sugar cube or two. Originals can still be found, and reproductions are becoming commonplace, so you can go vintage or faux, depending on how hard you want to look. The crown jewel of the traditional absinthe ritual is the fountain. If the spoons were ornate, the fountains—with their etched glass bowls and plated-brass spigots—were over the top, their resplendence a testament to absinthe's exalted status. Originals are still available at a price, but well-made reproductions also make great showpieces.

50 WAYS TO MIX WITH THE GREEN FAIRY

CHAPTER

THREE

the
CLASSICS

With its potent burst of alpine herbs and flirty natural sweetness, absinthe charmed many a bartender in its day. The recipes in this chapter represent the most beloved absinthe cocktails of all time, those so timeless that they survived the ninety-year drought. When the green fairy was reintroduced a few years ago, nostalgic cocktailians celebrated with these classic recipes—from stoic Sazeracs to punchy Monkey Glands and elegant Remember the Maines. Queue the cabaret tunes, the salon music, the jazz, the vaudeville, and sip one of these bibulous time machines.

Absinthe Drip

This isn't really a cocktail—it's the traditional way to prepare a glass of absinthe. If you haven't tasted absinthe before, try it this way before jumping into cocktail-making, to get a feel for the stuff. Whether you use sugar, and how much, is entirely a matter of individual taste. Premium absinthe does have bitter notes, and sugar has historically been a part of the absinthe ritual, but some find the spirit to be sweet enough on its own. Whatever you do, don't forget the water; in addition to tempering the strength of an absinthe, it opens up its flavors and really completes it.

1 OUNCE ABSINTHE

1 SUGAR CUBE OR
1 TEASPOON GRANULATED SUGAR (OPTIONAL)

5 OUNCES WATER, ICE-COLD

Pour the absinthe into an absinthe glass, wineglass, or water goblet. If using sugar, place an absinthe spoon or a small strainer across the top of the glass. Place the sugar on top of the spoon. Using a carafe, pitcher, or absinthe fountain slowly drizzle the water over the sugar and into the glass (or directly into the glass, if no sugar is desired). As the water mingles with the anise oils, the absinthe will begin to *louche* or cloud up, turning an ethereal pearly white.

MAKES 1 DRINK

This 5:1 water-absinthe ratio assumes an absinthe with a bottled strength of 68 percent alcohol by volume. If the absinthe you're using has a lower percentage of alcohol, or is mild in flavor, use less water. If your tap water's not great, or if you want to taste an absinthe unaltered by additional minerals, use purified water.

Absinthe Frappé

This most simple of absinthe cocktails is also one of the oldest and most refreshing on a hot day—hence its popularity in balmy nineteenth-century New Orleans. Sip slowly, so as not to freeze your brain.

1½ OUNCES ABSINTHE

½ OUNCE SIMPLE SYRUP

1 DASH BÉNÉDICTINE (OPTIONAL)

2 OUNCES SELTZER/SODA WATER, CHILLED

Pack a tall, narrow chimney glass with crushed ice. Add the absinthe, simple syrup, and the Bénédictine (if using). Stir to combine. Top with the seltzer/soda water.

MAKES 1 DRINK

In pre-Prohibition St. Louis, esteemed barman Tom Bullock dosed his frappés with a teaspoon of Bénédictine, an herbal, slightly sweet liqueur invented 500 years ago by monks. To some palates, and depending on the quality of the absinthe used, it may be an unnecessary addition, but others welcome the extra layer of depth.

Absinthe Suissesse

In New Orleans, this absinthe milkshake is still considered a brunch drink, but it's tasty any time of day. It's traditionally made with orgeat, an almond-based syrup. At the city's celebrated Swizzle Stick Bar, spunky bartendrix Lu Brow spices things up with her housemade orgeat punch.

1½ OUNCES ABSINTHE

½ OUNCE ORGEAT SYRUP OR LU BROW'S ORGEAT PUNCH (RECIPE FOLLOWS)

½ OUNCE HALF-AND-HALF/ HALF CREAM

1 EGG WHITE

½ CUP/100 G CRUSHED ICE

Fill a rocks glass with ice and let sit to chill. In a shaker, combine the absinthe, orgeat syrup, half-and-half/half cream, and egg white and shake to blend. Add the crushed ice and shake vigorously to chill. Discard the ice from the rocks glass, shaking out excess water. Pour the contents of the shaker into the chilled glass.

MAKES 1 DRINK

Lu Brow's Orgeat Punch

1 OUNCE ORGEAT SYRUP

1½ OUNCES SPICED RUM

½ OUNCE 151-PROOF RUM

½ OUNCE LIMONCELLO

½ OUNCE FRESHLY SQUEEZED LEMON JUICE

½ OUNCE FRESHLY SQUEEZED LIME JUICE

Combine the ingredients in a shaker or a bottle with a tight-fitting lid and shake to blend. Store leftover punch in the refrigerator for up to 2 days.

MAKES 4½ OUNCES

Sazerac

This is the granddaddy of absinthe cocktails. New Orleans pharmacist Antoine Peychaud first whipped up his proprietary mixture of cognac and bitters in the mid-nineteenth century. It eventually evolved into a whiskey drink with a signature absinthe rinse. To this day, you can walk into just about any bar in New Orleans and get a Sazerac. This particular recipe comes from Chris Hannah of the French 75 Bar, one of the city's most revered cocktail spots.

5 DASHES PEYCHAUD'S BITTERS

2 SUGAR CUBES OR 2 TEASPOONS SIMPLE SYRUP

2 OUNCES RYE WHISKEY

½ OUNCE ABSINTHE

GARNISH: LEMON PEEL

Fill a rocks glass with ice and let sit to chill. In a mixing glass, muddle the bitters and sugar cubes. Add the rye whiskey and stir with ice until chilled. Discard the ice from the rocks glass, shaking out excess water. Pour the absinthe into the chilled rocks glass, turning the glass to cover the surface. Discard excess absinthe, leaving a shallow puddle in the bottom of the glass. Strain the contents of the mixing glass into the absinthe-rinsed glass. Twist a strip of lemon peel over the drink and place it in the glass.

MAKES 1 DRINK

If you order a Sazerac at the French 75 Bar or almost any other bar in New Orleans, the bartender will use Herbsaint instead of absinthe. Herbsaint is a pastis created in New Orleans seventy-five years ago as an absinthe substitute. By the time absinthe was reintroduced in 2007, Herbsaint-rinsed Sazeracs were local tradition. Herbsaint is a quality product, but if you'd prefer an absinthe-rinsed Sazerac, just ask the bartender. Most will oblige.

Chrysanthemum

With all the herbs going on in this cocktail—from the lovely sixteenth-century liqueur Bénédictine to the wine- and herb-based vermouth to, not least, the absinthe—it's amazing that it tastes as light and elegant as its name suggests.

1½ OUNCES DOLIN BLANC OR ANOTHER BLANC OR BIANCO VERMOUTH

¾ OUNCE BÉNÉDICTINE

½ TEASPOON MARTEAU OR ANOTHER ABSINTHE VERTE

GARNISH: ORANGE PEEL OR EDIBLE FLOWERS (OPTIONAL)

Stir the ingredients with ice to chill. Strain into a stemmed glass. Twist a swath of orange peel over the drink, then place it in the glass.

MAKES 1 DRINK

Traditionally, at least as early as the 1920s, Chrysanthemums were made with dry vermouth. This adaptation by Daniel Shoemaker, helmer of the Teardrop Lounge in Portland, Oregon, is nice with a slightly sweet blanc or bianco vermouth.

Monkey Gland

That this cocktail remains popular despite its unappetizing name is evidence of its deliciousness. Its moniker refers to the peculiar science of Dr. Serge Abrahamovitch Voronoff, whose primate-to-human tissue-grafting experiments were all the rage for a brief moment in 1920s France.

1½ OUNCES DRY GIN

1½ OUNCES FRESHLY SQUEEZED ORANGE JUICE

1 TEASPOON JACKSON CANNON'S GRENADINE (RECIPE FOLLOWS)

6 DROPS ABSINTHE

GARNISH: BRANDIED CHERRY AND AN ORANGE SLICE, SPEARED TOGETHER ON A TOOTHPICK

Pour the ingredients into a shaker, add ice, and shake until chilled. Strain into a stemmed glass. Garnish.

MAKES 1 DRINK

Jackson Cannon's Grenadine

1 CUP/240 ML PURE POMEGRANATE JUICE

½ CUP/100 G SUGAR

1 DASH ORANGE FLOWER WATER

Combine the pomegranate juice and sugar in a saucepan and bring to a simmer over medium heat. Let simmer for about 5 minutes, stirring occasionally. Remove from the heat and set aside to cool. Finish with a dash of orange flower water. Store extra syrup in a covered container in the refrigerator. Keeps well for up to 2 weeks.

MAKES ABOUT 1 CUP/240 ML

Pan-American Clipper

In his 1939 cocktail guide, thirsty adventurer Charles Baker wrote of a pilot friend with a taste for this apple of a drink. Fortunately, the pilot only indulged while off duty. This adaptation comes from Erik Adkins at Heaven's Dog in San Francisco, whose bar menu is based entirely on Baker's drinks.

2 OUNCES CALVADOS OR APPLEJACK

½ OUNCE FRESHLY SQUEEZED LEMON JUICE

½ OUNCE JACKSON CANNON'S GRENADINE (FACING PAGE)

¼ TEASPOON DUPLAIS OR ANOTHER ABSINTHE VERTE

Combine the ingredients in a shaker with ice and shake until chilled. Strain into a stemmed glass.

MAKES 1 DRINK

Remember the Maine

In his cult-favorite 1939 drinking memoir, globetrotting writer Charles Baker remembers sipping this cocktail in Havana in 1933, mutiny underway, "each swallow . . . punctuated with bombs going off on the Prado." Its name reveals the still-smoldering resentment felt thirty-five years after the Spanish-American War. This adaptation comes from Julie Reiner, owner of Brooklyn's Clover Club. In a rebellion of her own, she replaces Baker's stemmed coupe with a sturdy rocks glass.

2½ OUNCES RYE WHISKEY

¾ OUNCE PUNT E MES OR ANOTHER SWEET VERMOUTH

¼ OUNCE CHERRY HEERING

ABSINTHE TO COAT THE GLASS

GARNISH: LEMON PEEL (OR BRANDIED CHERRY)

Fill a rocks glass with ice and let sit to chill. In a mixing glass, combine the rye, vermouth, and Cherry Heering and stir with ice until chilled. Discard the ice from the rocks glass, shaking out excess water. Pour just enough absinthe to coat the chilled rocks glass, turning the glass to cover the surface. Pour out any excess absinthe. Strain the contents of the mixing glass into the absinthe-rinsed glass. Twist a swath of lemon peel over the drink and place it in the glass.

MAKES 1 DRINK

Attention

Ethereal in color and in taste, this handsome cocktail does indeed attract attention. This adaptation of the Prohibition-era classic is a favorite of Seattle barman Jamie Boudreau.

2 OUNCES DRY GIN

¼ OUNCE ABSINTHE

¼ OUNCE DRY VERMOUTH

¼ OUNCE CRÈME DE VIOLETTE

2 DASHES ORANGE BITTERS

GARNISH: LEMON PEEL

Stir the ingredients with ice to chill. Strain into a stemmed glass. Twist a swath of lemon peel over the drink and place it in the glass.

MAKES 1 DRINK

If you think this cocktail is to die for, you might also like the classic Obituary, made with 2 ounces gin, ¼ ounce absinthe, and ¼ ounce dry vermouth. Simply follow the instructions for the Attention but let the violet liqueur and the orange bitters rest in peace.

Waldorf

This drink is named for New York's old Waldorf-Astoria Hotel, which sat where the Empire State Building now stands. This straightforward adaptation of the classic recipe comes from Seattle "cocktail whisperer" Jamie Boudreau.

¾ OUNCE BOURBON

¾ OUNCE ABSINTHE

¾ OUNCE SWEET VERMOUTH

3 DASHES ANGOSTURA OR OTHER AROMATIC BITTERS

Fill a stemmed glass with ice and let sit to chill. In a mixing glass, combine the ingredients and add ice, stirring briskly to chill. Discard the ice from the stemmed glass, shaking out excess water. Strain the contents of the mixing glass into the chilled glass.

MAKES 1 DRINK

Sea Fizz

In his 1946 *Stork Club Bar Book*, Lucius Beebe called this a breakfast drink. An egg, some lemon juice—the man's got a point. Whether you're imbibing before noon or after dark, this absinthe fizz will put some pep in your step.

1½ OUNCES ABSINTHE

¾ OUNCE FRESHLY SQUEEZED LEMON JUICE

½ OUNCE SIMPLE SYRUP

1 EGG WHITE

2 OUNCES SELTZER/SODA WATER, CHILLED

Fill a juice glass or a highball with ice and let sit to chill. In a shaker, combine the absinthe, lemon juice, simple syrup, and egg white and shake to blend. Add ice and shake until chilled. Add the seltzer/soda water and stir. Discard the ice from the glass, shaking out excess water. Strain the contents of the shaker into the chilled glass.

MAKES 1 DRINK

Morning Glory Fizz

Like the Sea Fizz (page 43), this nineteenth-century holdover was once considered a breakfast drink. The addition of scotch is a happy one. *Guid Mornin*!

1½ OUNCES SCOTCH

¾ OUNCE FRESHLY SQUEEZED LEMON JUICE

½ OUNCE SIMPLE SYRUP

¼ TEASPOON ABSINTHE

1 EGG WHITE

1 OUNCE SELTZER/SODA WATER, CHILLED

GARNISH: 1 DASH ANGOSTURA OR OTHER AROMATIC BITTERS

Fill a small juice glass or a highball with ice and let sit to chill. In a shaker, combine the scotch, lemon juice, simple syrup, absinthe, and egg white and shake to blend. Add ice and shake until chilled. Add the seltzer/soda water and stir. Discard the ice from the glass, shaking out excess water. Strain the contents of the shaker into the chilled glass. Dash the bitters on top.

MAKES 1 DRINK

Corpse Reviver No. 2

In the nineteenth and early twentieth centuries, morning-after tonics like this one were thought to revive and refresh a ragged mind after a night of drinking. Rinse, spin, repeat. The Savoy's Harry Craddock prescribed "four of these taken in swift succession" to weary revelers. No wonder the average life expectancy was under sixty. Please, start with just one.

¾ OUNCE DRY GIN

¾ OUNCE COINTREAU OR TRIPLE SEC

¾ OUNCE LILLET BLANC

¾ OUNCE FRESHLY SQUEEZED LEMON JUICE

8 DROPS ABSINTHE

GARNISH: BRANDIED CHERRY

Fill a stemmed glass with ice and let sit to chill. In a shaker, combine the ingredients and shake with ice until chilled. Discard the ice from the stemmed glass, shaking out excess water. Strain the contents of the shaker into the chilled glass. Garnish.

MAKES 1 DRINK

Modern

This recipe comes from the notebook of esteemed booze historian Ted "Dr. Cocktail" Haigh. In a brilliant turn, he updated the original Modern cocktail with a touch of smoky Swedish punsch, a unique Scandinavian liqueur. In his book *Vintage Spirits and Forgotten Cocktails,* he dubs it the Modernista. You might also call it the Post-Modern.

2 OUNCES SCOTCH

½ OUNCE AGED RUM

½ OUNCE SWEDISH PUNSCH

½ OUNCE FRESHLY SQUEEZED LEMON JUICE

1 TEASPOON ABSINTHE

2 DASHES ORANGE BITTERS

GARNISH: LEMON PEEL

In a shaker, combine the ingredients and shake with ice until chilled. Strain into a stemmed glass. Twist a swath of lemon peel over the drink and place it in the glass.

MAKES 1 DRINK

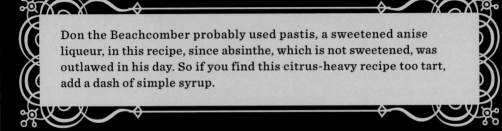

Don the Beachcomber probably used pastis, a sweetened anise liqueur, in this recipe, since absinthe, which is not sweetened, was outlawed in his day. So if you find this citrus-heavy recipe too tart, add a dash of simple syrup.

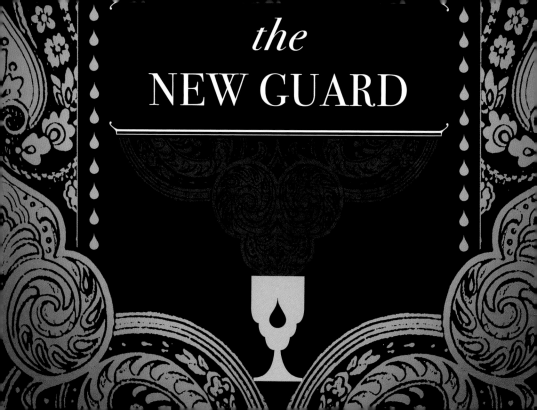

Absinthe, the emerald muse, famously inspired French painters and poets before it was banned. Now that it's back, it's inspiring another type of artist: bartenders. The top drink builders in the craft are once again lacing their creations with absinthe, ever seeking to harness its seductive herbal notes. Their attempts aren't always successful; characterful absinthe can be a difficult spirit to balance. But when absinthe cocktails are good, they're very, very good, and the recipes in this chapter represent the best in show. Some are based firmly on the classics; others are completely forward-thinking. All can be re-created at home, for casual pre-dinner sipping, elegant cocktail parties, and any occasion in between. Grab your shaker and follow along as some of the most talented bartenders in the world share their favorite recipes.

Continued

Tequila Sazerac

CHARLES VEXENAT, THE LONSDALE, LONDON

One of the biggest surprises of the post-ban absinthe cocktail phenomenon has been the green fairy's affinity for tequila. The two spirits harmonize beautifully. This playful nod to the Sazerac is unforgettable with a good, smoky tequila.

2 OUNCES TEQUILA AÑEJO

¼ TO ½ OUNCE CHARLES VEXENAT'S AGAVE SYRUP (FACING PAGE)

2 DASHES PEYCHAUD'S BITTERS

ABSINTHE TO COAT THE GLASS

GARNISH: LIME PEEL

Fill a rocks glass with ice and let sit to chill. In a mixing glass, stir the tequila, agave syrup, and bitters with ice until chilled. Discard the ice from the rocks glass, shaking out excess water. Pour just enough absinthe to coat the inside of the glass, turning the glass to cover the surface. Pour out any excess absinthe. Strain the contents of the mixing glass into the absinthe-rinsed glass. Twist a swath of lime peel over the drink and place it in the glass.

MAKES 1 DRINK

Charles Vexenat's Agave Syrup

1 CUP/240 ML AGAVE NECTAR

½ CUP/120 ML WATER

Combine the agave nectar and water in a bottle with a tight-fitting lid. Cover and shake to combine. Store leftover syrup in the refrigerator. Keeps well for up to 2 weeks.

MAKES 1½ CUPS/360 ML SYRUP

Agave nectar is made from the same plant that tequila is distilled from. It's a delicious sweetener, and especially befitting of tequila drinks. Charles Vexenat's agave syrup, a mixture of agave nectar and water, is very easy to make. For fun, try it in other cocktails in place of simple syrup. It's also handy for sweetening iced coffee and tea. Agave is sweeter than table sugar, so start small and sweeten to taste.

Judgment Day

CHARLES VEXENAT, THE LONSDALE, LONDON

Created with gratitude for a friend who helped Vexenat out of a sticky situation, this jazzed up tribute to Peru's national cocktail—the pisco sour—is appropriately complex, yet rewarding.

¾ OUNCE PLUS ½ TEASPOON PISCO, SUCH AS MACCHU PISCO

¾ OUNCE PLUS ½ TEASPOON ST. GERMAIN ELDERFLOWER LIQUEUR

⅓ OUNCE FRESHLY SQUEEZED LIME JUICE

⅓ OUNCE FRESHLY SQUEEZED LEMON JUICE

1 TEASPOON SIMPLE SYRUP

1 EGG WHITE

½ TEASPOON ABSINTHE

GARNISH: 4 DROPS OR A SPRAY OF PIMENTO DRAM LIQUEUR

In a shaker, combine the ingredients and shake without ice to blend. Add ice and shake until chilled. Strain into a stemmed glass. Top with the pimento dram.

MAKES 1 DRINK

Déjà vu

RICCARDO SEMERIA, CONNAUGHT BAR, LONDON

During Prohibition, American bartenders like Harry Craddock took their craft to Europe. At London's Savoy Hotel, Craddock earned a following for cocktails like the Bombay No. 2, which was made with brandy, sweet and dry vermouths, and dashes of absinthe and curaçao. Here's a nod to that drink, almost a century later, from another London barman.

ABSINTHE TO COAT THE GLASS, PLUS 3 DROPS

1⅓ OUNCES ARMAGNAC OR COGNAC

⅓ OUNCE NOILLY PRAT OR ANOTHER DRY VERMOUTH

½ OUNCE BÉNÉDICTINE

GARNISH: ORANGE PEEL

In a stemmed glass, pour just enough absinthe to coat the inside, turning the glass to cover the surface. Pour out any excess absinthe. In a shaker, combine the 3 drops absinthe, armagnac, vermouth, and Bénédictine and shake with ice until chilled. Strain into the absinthe-rinsed glass. Twist a swath of orange peel over the drink and place it in the glass.

MAKES 1 DRINK

Reverse Sazerac Sour

ALES OLASZ, MONTGOMERY PLACE, LONDON

English bartenders have a lot of fun with themes and concepts. This recipe turns the Sazerac inside out and fashions it into a sour. It's a potent, gutsy drink, and entirely seductive. It's best with a good, smoky single-malt scotch.

SCOTCH TO COAT THE GLASS

1⅓ OUNCES ABSINTHE

½ OUNCE PLUS 1 TEASPOON FRESHLY SQUEEZED LEMON JUICE

½ OUNCE PLUS 1 TEASPOON SIMPLE SYRUP

1 EGG WHITE

GARNISH: LEMON PEEL AND 3 DASHES PEYCHAUD'S BITTERS

In a stemmed glass, pour just enough scotch to coat the inside, turning the glass to cover the surface. Pour out any excess scotch. In a shaker, combine the remaining ingredients and shake without ice to blend. Add ice and shake until chilled. Strain into the scotch-rinsed glass. Twist a swath of lemon peel over the drink, and season the rim of the drink with it. Dash the bitters on top.

MAKES 1 DRINK

Stargazer

JIM MEEHAN, PDT, NEW YORK

Not vacationing on Mauritius this year? One can dream, and this absinthe-laced spin-off of the classic East India cocktail will take you halfway. The island's volcanic soil makes Starr African Rum one-of-a-kind, but in a pinch, substitute a white agricole-style rum from the islands of Martinique or Guadalupe.

1½ OUNCES STARR AFRICAN RUM

¾ OUNCE FRESHLY PRESSED PINEAPPLE JUICE

½ OUNCE KIRSCHWASSER CHERRY BRANDY

¼ OUNCE APEROL

¼ OUNCE VIEUX PONTARLIER OR ANOTHER ABSINTHE VERTE

Fill a stemmed glass with ice and let sit to chill. In a shaker, combine the ingredients and shake with ice until chilled. Discard the ice from the stemmed glass, shaking out excess water. Strain the contents of the shaker into the chilled glass.

MAKES 1 DRINK

Shiso Malt Sour

JIM MEEHAN, PDT, NEW YORK

Kyoto-born Yamazaki whisky headlines this zesty homage to Japan's fashionable cocktail culture. If you don't have Japanese whisky on hand, a 12-year-old Scotch whisky would be a suitable—though considerably less thematic—alternative. Fresh shiso leaves, sometimes called Japanese mint, can be found at Asian markets.

3 FRESH SHISO LEAVES

¾ OUNCE SIMPLE SYRUP

2 OUNCES YAMAZAKI 12-YEAR-OLD SINGLE-MALT WHISKY

¾ OUNCE FRESHLY SQUEEZED LIME JUICE

¼ OUNCE VIEUX PONTARLIER OR ANOTHER ABSINTHE VERTE

1 EGG WHITE

Fill a stemmed glass with ice and let sit to chill. In a shaker, muddle 2 of the shiso leaves and the simple syrup. Add the whisky, lime juice, absinthe, and egg white and shake without ice to blend. Add ice and shake until chilled. Discard the ice from the stemmed glass, shaking out excess water. Strain the contents of the shaker into the chilled glass. Garnish with the remaining shiso leaf.

MAKES 1 DRINK

El Burro

JIM MEEHAN, PDT, NEW YORK

This inspired cousin to the tequila mule has a nice kick. At PDT, house-made ginger beer makes it extra special. As a stand-in, Meehan recommends a spicy brand like Barritt's, Stewart's, or Europe's Belvoir.

1½ OUNCES TEQUILA REPOSADO

¾ OUNCE FRESHLY SQUEEZED LIME JUICE

¾ OUNCE FRESHLY PRESSED PINEAPPLE JUICE

½ OUNCE SIMPLE SYRUP

¼ OUNCE VIEUX PONTARLIER OR ANOTHER ABSINTHE VERTE

1 OUNCE GINGER BEER

GARNISH: LIME WHEEL AND A CANDIED GINGER SLICE, SKEWERED TOGETHER ON A TOOTHPICK

Fill a tall glass with ice cubes. In a shaker, combine all of the ingredients except the ginger beer and shake with ice until chilled. Strain the contents of the shaker into the ice-filled tall glass. Top with ginger beer. Garnish.

MAKES 1 DRINK

Benjamin Barker Daiquiri

BRIAN MILLER, DEATH AND COMPANY, NEW YORK

Here's an absinthe-laced twist on a classic rum cocktail. This blood-red daiquiri may be named after a knife-wielding barber, but the flavor is delightful.

2 OUNCES AGED RUM

½ OUNCE CAMPARI

½ OUNCE FRESHLY SQUEEZED LIME JUICE

½ OUNCE DEMERARA-BASED SIMPLE SYRUP

⅛ TEASPOON VIEUX PONTARLIER OR ANOTHER ABSINTHE VERTE

GARNISH: LIME WHEEL

In a shaker, combine the ingredients and shake with ice until chilled. Strain into a stemmed glass. Float the lime wheel on top.

MAKES 1 DRINK

My Oh My Ty

BRIAN MILLER, DEATH AND COMPANY, NEW YORK

Absinthe meets the mai tai meets the French Caribbean in this tiki-fabulous cooler. Absinthe and rum are old friends (see Doctor Funk, page 49), and this drink's almond and orange elements are gorgeous with the anise-forward spirit.

1 OUNCE AGED RUM

1 OUNCE WHITE RHUM AGRICOLE

1 OUNCE FRESHLY SQUEEZED LIME JUICE

½ OUNCE CLÉMENT CRÉOLE SHRUBB ORANGE LIQUEUR

½ OUNCE ORGEAT SYRUP

¼ OUNCE VIEUX PONTARLIER OR ANOTHER ABSINTHE VERTE

⅛ OUNCE SIMPLE SYRUP

GARNISH: LARGE SPRIG OF MINT

Pack a tall glass or tiki coconut mug with crushed ice. In a shaker, combine the ingredients with three ice cubes and shake until chilled. Strain into the ice-filled tall glass. Garnish.

MAKES 1 DRINK

Amore Morado

PHIL WARD, MAYAHUEL, NEW YORK

True to its name—"violet love"—this amethyst beauty might run off with your heart. It celebrates the revival of three vintage ingredients, not just absinthe but also tart, fruity sloe gin and floral crème de violette liqueur.

1 OUNCE TEQUILA BLANCO

1 OUNCE SLOE GIN

¾ OUNCE FRESHLY SQUEEZED GRAPEFRUIT JUICE

½ OUNCE FRESHLY SQUEEZED LEMON JUICE

½ OUNCE SIMPLE SYRUP

¼ OUNCE CRÈME DE VIOLETTE

⅓ TEASPOON VIEUX PONTARLIER OR ANOTHER ABSINTHE VERTE

GARNISH: EDIBLE VIOLET, PLAIN OR SUGARED

In a shaker, combine the ingredients and shake with ice until chilled. Strain into a stemmed glass. Garnish.

MAKES 1 DRINK

Gill Sans

JEFF HOLLINGER, ABSINTHE BRASSERIE, SAN FRANCISCO

Absinthe plays a pivotal supporting role in this deft salute to the Martinez cocktail, a nineteenth-century predecessor to the martini.

2 OUNCES CUCUMBER-FORWARD GIN, SUCH AS HENDRICK'S

¾ OUNCE MANZANILLA SHERRY

¼ OUNCE MARASCHINO LIQUEUR

2 DASHES ORANGE BITTERS

ABSINTHE TO COAT THE GLASS

GARNISH: LEMON PEEL

Fill a stemmed glass with ice and let sit to chill. In a mixing glass, combine the gin, sherry, maraschino liqueur, and bitters and stir with ice until chilled. Discard the ice from the stemmed glass, shaking out excess water. Pour just enough absinthe to coat the inside of the chilled glass, turning the glass to cover the surface. Pour out any excess absinthe. Strain the contents of the mixing glass into the chilled, absinthe-rinsed glass. Twist a swath of lemon peel over the drink and place it in the glass.

MAKES 1 DRINK

Night Porter

JEFF HOLLINGER, ABSINTHE BRASSERIE, SAN FRANCISCO

This is an intense, sophisticated drink from a fellow quite familiar with absinthian allure (his bar is named for the stuff). The unique Spanish absinthe Obsello finds worthy matches in charismatic mescal and port.

1 OUNCE DOLIN BLANC OR ANOTHER BLANC OR BIANCO VERMOUTH

¾ OUNCE OBSELLO OR ANOTHER ABSINTHE VERTE

¾ OUNCE RUBY PORT

½ OUNCE MESCAL

GARNISH: LEMON PEEL OR WHEEL

Fill a stemmed glass with ice and let sit to chill. In a mixing glass, combine the ingredients and stir with ice until chilled. Discard the ice from the stemmed glass, shaking out excess water. Strain the contents of the mixing glass into the chilled glass. Twist a swath of lemon peel over the drink and place it in the glass.

MAKES 1 DRINK

Promissory Note

DANIEL HYATT, THE ALEMBIC, SAN FRANCISCO

Ginger and anise harmonize sweetly in this multidimensional cocktail. It's golden with a rich, woodsy tequila.

¾ OUNCE REPOSADO TEQUILA

¾ OUNCE DRY VERMOUTH

1 OUNCE DOMAINE DE CANTON GINGER LIQUEUR

1 TEASPOON HONEY

8 DROPS ABSINTHE

GARNISH: LIME PEEL, RADISH SLICE, AND PINCH OF GROUND CINNAMON

Fill a stemmed glass with ice and let sit to chill. In a mixing glass, combine the ingredients and stir with ice until chilled. Discard the ice from the stemmed glass, shaking out excess water. Strain the contents of the mixing glass into the chilled glass. Twist a swath of lime peel over the drink, then discard. Float a radish slice and dust with ground cinnamon.

MAKES 1 DRINK

Dolores Park Swizzle

THAD VOGLER, BAR AGRICOLE, SAN FRANCISCO

Vogler dusts off an early tiki-bar drink—the Trinidad-born Queen's Park Swizzle—and adds a dynamic duo: absinthe and maraschino cherry liqueur. Be careful with this one, it's altogether too tasty.

2 OUNCES WHITE RHUM AGRICOLE

1 OUNCE FRESHLY SQUEEZED LIME JUICE

½ OUNCE MARTINIQUE CANE SYRUP/LYLE'S GOLDEN SYRUP OR DEMERARA-BASED SIMPLE SYRUP

¼ OUNCE MARASCHINO LIQUEUR

¼ TEASPOON ST. GEORGE OR ANOTHER ABSINTHE VERTE

GARNISH: LARGE SPRIG OF MINT AND 3 DASHES PEYCHAUD'S BITTERS

Pack a tall narrow glass with crushed ice. Pour in the ingredients and stir. Garnish with the mint and bitters.

MAKES 1 DRINK

Strawberry's Revival

BRIAN MacGREGOR, JARDINIÈRE, SAN FRANCISCO

Rye whiskey lends a subtle spice to this fruity summer sipper. Fresh strawberries get a boost from absinthe's sweet anise and alpine herbs.

1 TO 2 MEDIUM STRAWBERRIES, HULLED AND QUARTERED

1½ OUNCES RYE WHISKEY

¾ OUNCE FRESHLY SQUEEZED LEMON JUICE

½ OUNCE VIEUX PONTARLIER OR ANOTHER ABSINTHE VERTE

½ OUNCE MARTINIQUE CANE SYRUP/LYLE'S GOLDEN SYRUP OR DEMERARA-BASED SIMPLE SYRUP

2 DASHES ANGOSTURA BITTERS

In a shaker, muddle the strawberry pieces well. Add the remaining ingredients and shake with ice until chilled. Pour the contents of the shaker, unstrained, into a large rocks glass.

MAKES 1 DRINK

Count's Fancy

ERIC ALPERIN, THE VARNISH, LOS ANGELES

Absinthe makes the heart grow fonder—of the classic negroni cocktail. Even if gin, Campari, and sweet vermouth seem to you a holy trinity that needs no updating, you might be pleasantly surprised.

KÜBLER OR ANOTHER ABSINTHE BLANCHE TO COAT THE GLASS

1 OUNCE DRY GIN

1 OUNCE CAMPARI

1 OUNCE DOLIN ROUGE OR ANOTHER SWEET VERMOUTH

ORANGE PEEL

In a stemmed glass, pour just enough absinthe to coat the inside, turning the glass to cover the surface. Pour out any excess absinthe. In a mixing glass, combine the remaining ingredients, except the orange peel, and stir with ice until chilled. Strain into the absinthe-rinsed glass. Hold a lit match a couple of inches above the drink. With the other hand, squeeze a swath of orange peel, skin-side down, over the match to release its oils into the drink. The oil will ignite briefly when it passes through the flame, caramelizing slightly. Discard the peel.

MAKES 1 DRINK

La Lucha Sigue

CHRIS BOSTICK, THE VARNISH, LOS ANGELES

The name means "the struggle continues," but there's no sign of conflict in this sturdy cocktail—brawny as the ingredients are, it's a meeting of equals.

1¾ OUNCES TEQUILA AÑEJO

¾ OUNCE SWEET VERMOUTH

¼ OUNCE NONINO OR ANOTHER ITALIAN AMARO

¼ OUNCE KÜBLER OR ANOTHER ABSINTHE BLANCHE

3 DASHES ORANGE BITTERS

GARNISH: ORANGE PEEL

Fill a stemmed glass with ice and let sit to chill. In a mixing glass, combine the ingredients and stir until chilled. Discard the ice from the stemmed glass, shaking out excess water. Strain the contents of the mixing glass into the chilled glass. Twist a swath of orange peel over the drink and place it in the glass.

MAKES 1 DRINK

Absinthe 75

MARCOS TELLO, THE EDISON AND THE VARNISH, LOS ANGELES

Absinthe stands in for gin in this herbal, anise-forward play on the classic French 75.

1 OUNCE KÜBLER OR ANOTHER ABSINTHE BLANCHE

¾ OUNCE FRESHLY SQUEEZED LEMON JUICE

¾ OUNCE SIMPLE SYRUP

2 TO 3 OUNCES SPARKLING WINE, CHILLED

GARNISH: LEMON PEEL

In a shaker, combine the absinthe, lemon juice, and simple syrup and shake with ice until chilled. Strain into a flute and top with sparkling wine. Twist a long strip of lemon peel over the drink and place it in the glass.

MAKES 1 DRINK

La Belle Femme

CHRIS HANNAH, FRENCH 75 BAR, NEW ORLEANS

A rich, flirtatious number named, as Hannah likes to say, for the beautiful women of the French Quarter.

1¾ OUNCES COGNAC OR ARMAGNAC

½ OUNCE DUBONNET ROUGE

⅓ OUNCE APEROL

¼ OUNCE MARTEAU OR ANOTHER ABSINTHE VERTE

GARNISH: ORANGE PEEL

Fill a stemmed glass with ice and let sit to chill. In a mixing glass, combine the ingredients and stir with ice until chilled. Discard the ice from the stemmed glass, shaking out excess water. Strain the contents of the mixing glass into the chilled glass. Twist a swath of orange peel over the drink and place it in the glass.

MAKES 1 DRINK

Necromancer

CHRIS HANNAH, FRENCH 75 BAR, NEW ORLEANS

Cocktail noir from the U.S. city that first embraced the mystique of *la fée verte*, this pretty-in-purple sipper is simple yet seductive.

1½ OUNCES MARTEAU OR ANOTHER ABSINTHE VERTE

½ OUNCE BOTTLED STILL WATER

½ OUNCE CRÈME YVETTE OR ANOTHER CRÈME DE VIOLETTE

GARNISH: 1 DASH PEYCHAUD'S BITTERS AND EDIBLE FLOWERS (OPTIONAL)

Fill a rocks glass with crushed ice. In a mixing glass combine the absinthe, water, and Crème Yvette with cracked or cubed ice and stir until chilled. Strain the contents of the mixing glass into the ice-filled rocks glass. Top with the bitters and flowers, if desired.

MAKES 1 DRINK

Cherry Blossom Brocade

CHRIS HANNAH, FRENCH 75 BAR, NEW ORLEANS

Absinthe opens up this fruity, herbaceous cocktail. It's named after a corset, but there's nothing restrictive about it.

1½ OUNCES GENEVER, A DUTCH GIN

1 OUNCE FRESHLY SQUEEZED RUBY RED GRAPEFRUIT JUICE

½ OUNCE CHERRY HEERING

¼ OUNCE MARTEAU OR ANOTHER ABSINTHE VERTE

GARNISH: FRESH CHERRY WITH STEM

Fill a stemmed glass with ice and let sit to chill. In a shaker, combine the ingredients and shake with ice until chilled. Discard the ice from the stemmed glass, shaking out excess water. Strain the contents of the shaker into the chilled glass. Garnish.

MAKES 1 DRINK

Absinthe and Old Lace

JACKSON CANNON, EASTERN STANDARD, BOSTON

A premium crème de menthe like Marie Brizard's makes this Grasshopper spin-off sing. Bittermens' revolutionary Xocolatl Mole Bitters are worth seeking out.

1 OUNCE DRY GIN

½ OUNCE ABSINTHE VERTE

½ OUNCE GREEN CRÈME DE MENTHE

½ OUNCE SIMPLE SYRUP

½ OUNCE HALF-AND-HALF/HALF CREAM

1 EGG WHITE

GARNISH: 1 DASH BITTERMENS' XOCOLATL MOLE BITTERS OR SHAVED BITTERSWEET CHOCOLATE

Fill a stemmed glass with ice and let sit to chill. In a shaker, combine the ingredients and shake without ice to blend. Add ice and shake until chilled. Discard the ice from the stemmed glass, shaking out excess water. Strain the contents of the shaker into the chilled glass. Top with the bitters.

MAKES 1 DRINK

This drink is similar in name to a classic absinthe cocktail, Arsenic and Old Lace. That one is nearly identical to the Attention (page 41), consisting of gin, absinthe, crème de violette, and dry vermouth.

Hotel Haute-Savoie

MISTY KALKOFEN, DRINK, BOSTON

This riff on the classic Lawhill cocktail, served at the Savoy in London in the 1920s, replaces maraschino liqueur with a floral, alpine elderflower liqueur—a worthy match for an herbal Swiss absinthe.

2 OUNCES RYE WHISKEY

1 OUNCE ST. GERMAIN ELDERFLOWER LIQUEUR

½ OUNCE NOILLY PRAT OR ANOTHER DRY VERMOUTH

1 TEASPOON KÜBLER OR ANOTHER ABSINTHE BLANCHE

1 DASH ANGOSTURA OR OTHER AROMATIC BITTERS

1 DASH ORANGE BITTERS

In a mixing glass, stir the ingredients with ice until chilled. Strain into a stemmed glass.

MAKES 1 DRINK

Learning to Tie

DAVE SHENAUT, TEARDROP LOUNGE, PORTLAND, OREGON

In this mai tai send-up, absinthe goes up against Brazilian sugarcane rum and bitter Campari—and everybody wins.

1¼ OUNCES CACHAÇA

1 OUNCE ORGEAT SYRUP

1 OUNCE FRESHLY SQUEEZED ORANGE JUICE

½ OUNCE PACIFIQUE OR ANOTHER ABSINTHE VERTE

½ TEASPOON CAMPARI

GARNISH: ORANGE PEEL

In a mixing glass, combine the ingredients and stir with ice until chilled. Strain into a stemmed glass. Tie a strip of orange peel into a loose knot and place it in the glass.

MAKES 1 DRINK

Sandcastles in the Sky

DANIEL SHOEMAKER, TEARDROP LOUNGE, PORTLAND, OREGON

This cocktail is all about the scotch—Shoemaker prefers a floral, lightly smoked Speyside scotch, like Glenfarclas—but the absinthe, Bénédictine, and an obscure French aperitif ensure this drink is anything but one-dimensional.

1½ OUNCES SINGLE-MALT SCOTCH

¾ OUNCE FLOC DE GASCOGNE BLANC

½ OUNCE BÉNÉDICTINE

1 DASH FEE'S OLD FASHION BITTERS

8 DROPS MARTEAU OR ANOTHER ABSINTHE VERTE

1 RIBBON OF LEMON PEEL

1 RIBBON OF ORANGE PEEL

In a mixing glass, combine the ingredients and stir with ice until chilled. Strain into a stemmed glass.

MAKES 1 DRINK

Minor Threat

EVAN ZIMMERMAN, LAURELHURST MARKET, PORTLAND, OREGON

Sweet anise and rugged wormwood shine through this lyrical mix. If you're substituting a standard gin—Hendrick's is infused with cucumber and rose petals—muddle a slice of cucumber in the shaker, and garnish the glass with another cucumber slice.

1 OUNCE APEROL

¾ OUNCE HENDRICK'S GIN

½ OUNCE FRESHLY SQUEEZED LEMON JUICE

¼ OUNCE ABSINTHE VERTE

1 EGG WHITE

6 DROPS ROSE WATER

GARNISH: 4 DROPS OR A SPRAY OF ABSINTHE

In a shaker, combine the ingredients and shake without ice to blend. Add ice and shake until chilled. Strain into a stemmed glass. Top with the 4 drops of absinthe.

MAKES 1 DRINK

L'amour en Fuite

JAMIE BOUDREAU, KNEE HIGH STOCKING CO., SEATTLE

This contemporary classic was one of the first cocktails to pair absinthe and St. Germain elderflower liqueur, kicking off what's sure to be a long love affair.

PACIFIQUE OR ANOTHER ABSINTHE VERTE TO COAT THE GLASS

1½ OUNCES DRY GIN

¾ OUNCE LILLET BLANC

¼ OUNCE ST. GERMAIN ELDERFLOWER LIQUEUR

In a stemmed glass, pour just enough absinthe to coat the inside, turning the glass to cover the surface. Pour out any excess absinthe. In a mixing glass, combine the remaining ingredients and stir with ice until chilled. Strain the contents of the mixing glass into the absinthe-rinsed glass.

MAKES 1 DRINK

Fifth Avenue

JIM ROMDALL, VESSEL, SEATTLE

An elegant soprano with a tone that's warm and sweet, even on the herbaceous high notes.

1½ OUNCES DRY GIN

½ OUNCE DOLIN BLANC OR ANOTHER BLANC OR BIANCO VERMOUTH

1 TEASPOON YELLOW CHARTREUSE

10 DROPS MARTEAU OR ANOTHER ABSINTHE VERTE

3 DASHES LEMON BITTERS

GARNISH: LEMON PEEL

In a mixing glass, combine the ingredients with ice and stir until chilled. Strain into a stemmed glass. Twist a swath of lemon peel over the drink and place it in the glass.

MAKES 1 DRINK

Rhythm and Soul

GREG BEST, HOLEMAN AND FINCH PUBLIC HOUSE, ATLANTA

A pleasingly bitter Italian amaro gives this love child of the Sazerac and the Manhattan a life of its own.

LEOPOLD BROTHERS OR ANOTHER ABSINTHE VERTE TO COAT THE GLASS

1½ OUNCES RYE WHISKEY

½ OUNCE AVERNA OR ANOTHER ITALIAN AMARO

½ OUNCE CARPANO ANTICA OR ANOTHER SWEET VERMOUTH

2 DASHES ANGOSTURA BITTERS

GARNISH: LEMON PEEL

In a rocks glass, pour just enough absinthe to coat the inside, turning the glass to cover the surface. Pour out any excess absinthe. In a mixing glass, combine the remaining ingredients and stir with ice until chilled. Strain the contents of the mixing glass into the absinthe-rinsed glass. Twist a swath of lemon peel over the drink and place it in the glass.

MAKES 1 DRINK

Re-Animator

GREG BEST, HOLEMAN AND FINCH PUBLIC HOUSE, ATLANTA

This riff on the Corpse Reviver No. 2 (page 47) turns up the volume on the green fairy. This is a good venue for showcasing a rich, complex absinthe like Spain's Obsello.

1 OUNCE OBSELLO OR ANOTHER ABSINTHE VERTE

1 OUNCE BLUE COAT, AVIATION, OR ANOTHER AMERICAN DRY GIN

1 OUNCE COINTREAU

1 TEASPOON FRESHLY SQUEEZED LEMON JUICE

Fill a stemmed glass with ice and let sit to chill. In a mixing glass, combine the ingredients and stir with ice until chilled. Discard the ice from the stemmed glass, shaking out excess water. Strain the contents of the mixing glass into the chilled glass.

MAKES 1 DRINK

Vincent's Ruin

TOBY MALONEY, THE PATTERSON HOUSE, NASHVILLE

Absinthe and its new sidekick, St. Germain, lend fanciful adornment to this bright, sturdy bourbon drink.

ABSINTHE VERTE TO COAT THE GLASS

2 OUNCES BOURBON

¾ OUNCE FRESHLY SQUEEZED LEMON JUICE

½ OUNCE ST. GERMAIN ELDERFLOWER LIQUEUR

¼ OUNCE SIMPLE SYRUP

13 DROPS LEMON BITTERS

GARNISH: LEMON PEEL

In a rocks glass, pour enough absinthe to coat the interior, turning the glass to cover the surface. Pour out any excess absinthe. In a shaker, combine the remaining ingredients and shake with ice until chilled. Strain the contents of the shaker into the absinthe-rinsed glass. Squeeze a large swath of lemon peel over the drink and place it in the glass.

MAKES 1 DRINK

Spring Sazerac

TOBY MALONEY, BRADSTREET CRAFTHOUSE, MINNEAPOLIS

This vernal cousin of the classic Bombay No. 2 and Sazerac cocktails reads like a lion on paper but goes down like a lamb.

KÜBLER OR ANOTHER ABSINTHE BLANCHE TO COAT THE GLASS

2 OUNCES COGNAC OR ARMAGNAC

⅛ OUNCE ORANGE CURAÇAO

⅛ OUNCE DEMERARA-BASED SIMPLE SYRUP

11 DROPS ORANGE BITTERS

9 DROPS ANGOSTURA OR OTHER AROMATIC BITTERS

LEMON PEEL

In a rocks glass, pour just enough absinthe to coat the interior, turning the glass to cover the surface. Pack the glass with ice. In a mixing glass, combine the remaining ingredients, except the lemon peel, and stir with ice until chilled. Discard the ice from the rocks glass, shaking out excess water and absinthe. Strain the contents of the mixing glass into the absinthe-rinsed glass. Twist a swath of lemon peel over the drink, season the rim of the glass with it, and discard.

MAKES 1 DRINK

Broken Shoe Shiner

TOBY MALONEY AND STEPHEN COLE, THE VIOLET HOUR, CHICAGO

This bright, herbalicious absinthe sour is greater than the sum of its parts.

¾ OUNCE KÜBLER OR ANOTHER ABSINTHE BLANCHE

1 OUNCE BÉNÉDICTINE

1 OUNCE APEROL

1 OUNCE FRESHLY SQUEEZED LEMON JUICE

1 OUNCE FRESHLY PRESSED PINEAPPLE JUICE

1 EGG WHITE

GARNISH: 3 DROPS ROSE WATER

In a shaker, combine the ingredients and shake without ice to blend. Add ice and shake until chilled. Strain into a stemmed glass. Top with the rose water.

The Sun Also Rises

CHARLES JOLY, THE DRAWING ROOM, CHICAGO

Here's a decidedly more quaffable drink than the hair-raising one that inspired it; Ernest Hemingway's infamous Death in the Afternoon cocktail was essentially a glass of champagne fortified with a jigger of absinthe. "Hemingway was definitely a better writer than mixologist— but one hell of a drinker," Joly notes.

4 OUNCES CHAMPAGNE OR ANOTHER SPARKLING WINE, CHILLED

¾ OUNCE SLOE GIN

½ OUNCE FRESHLY SQUEEZED LEMON JUICE

¼ OUNCE SIRÈNE OR ANOTHER ABSINTHE VERTE

¼ OUNCE SIMPLE SYRUP

GARNISH: 3 DASHES PEYCHAUD'S BITTERS

Pour the champagne into a flute. In a shaker, combine the remaining ingredients and shake with ice until chilled. Slowly strain the contents of the shaker into the champagne-filled flute. Top with the bitters.

MAKES 1 DRINK

Libertine

CHARLES JOLY, THE DRAWING ROOM, CHICAGO

This whimsical, aromatic cocktail pairs absinthe with a spicy, floral white wine and rich, melodious Carpano Antica vermouth.

1 OUNCE SIRÈNE OR ANOTHER ABSINTHE VERTE

1 OUNCE GEWÜRZTRAMINER

1 OUNCE CARPANO ANTICA OR ANOTHER SWEET VERMOUTH, PLUS 3 DROPS

¾ OUNCE FRESHLY SQUEEZED LIME JUICE

½ OUNCE SIMPLE SYRUP

3 DROPS ORANGE FLOWER WATER

GARNISH: EDIBLE FLOWERS

Fill a stemmed glass with ice. In a shaker, combine the absinthe, Gewürztraminer, 1 ounce vermouth, lime juice, and simple syrup and shake with ice until chilled. Discard the ice from the stemmed glass, shaking out excess water. Strain the contents of the shaker into the chilled glass. Top with the 3 drops vermouth and the orange flower water. Garnish.

MAKES 1 DRINK

Glossary

AMARO A category of bitter Italian digestive flavored with a variety of herbs, citrus peels, roots, barks, and spices. Notable brands include light and fruity Amaro Nonino and rich and brawny Averna.

ANISE One of the defining ingredients in absinthe. It's a naturally sweet herb with a distinctive licorice-like taste.

APEROL A bittersweet Italian aperitif distinguished by its bright orange color and astringent orange-peel flavor.

BELLE ÉPOQUE In France, the "beautiful era" of art and lavishness between approximately 1890 and 1914.

BRANDIED CHERRY A whole cherry macerated in brandy or a liqueur, with or without the stem and pit. This cocktail garnish is available at well-stocked spirits shops and imported-food markets. And it's easy to make brandied cherries at home—place cherries (preferably fresh but frozen works) in a jar and cover them with a brandy of your choice. Seal the jar tightly and store in the refrigerator.

CHERRY HEERING A classic, brandy-based cherry liqueur produced in Denmark. In a pinch, substitute a maraschino liqueur or a sweetened, cherry-flavored brandy.

CLÉMENT CRÉOLE SHRUBB A rum-based orange liqueur produced on the Caribbean island of Martinique.

CRÈME DE VIOLETTE A purple liqueur flavored with violets. The classic cocktail ingredient was recently made available again in the United States after a long dry spell. The most celebrated brand is Crème Yvette, which is enhanced by vanilla and other spices.

EMERALD MUSE A nickname for absinthe.

FENNEL A naturally sweet herb with a licorice-like flavor, similar to anise.

FLOC DE GASCOGNE A brandy-based aperitif made in the Armagnac region of France. A suitable substitute is Pineau des Charentes, another brandy-based aperitif that is more widely available.

GENEVER A traditional Dutch spirit flavored with juniper and other botanicals. It's often called Dutch gin or Holland gin, but it is not as dry as the more common English or American gins.

GREEN FAIRY A nickname for absinthe. In French, *la fée verte.*

GREEN GODDESS A nickname for absinthe.

GREEN HOUR A period of the day reserved for enjoying absinthe, similar to a happy hour. In French, *l'heure verte.*

KIRSCHWASSER A dry, colorless, cherry-flavored brandy native to Germany. American distiller Clear Creek makes an excellent version.

L'HEURE VERTE *See* Green Hour.

LOUCHE The milky, opalescent transformation that absinthe undergoes when water is added.

PASTIS An anise-based absinthe substitute. Unlike absinthe, it's sweetened slightly before bottling, and it lacks wormwood, a defining ingredient in absinthe. Herbsaint is a recommended brand.

PIMENTO DRAM A spicy, rum-based Jamaican liqueur flavored with pimento berries or allspice.

THUJONE A chemical compound found in wormwood and other herbs, such as common sage. In large quantities, it has been shown to cause convulsions in lab animals. It exists in absinthe only in trace amounts.

WORMWOOD A bitter, woody herb that is a defining ingredient in absinthe.

Liquid Measures

Bar spoon = ½ ounce

1 teaspoon = ⅙ ounce

1 tablespoon = ½ ounce

2 tablespoons (pony) = 1 ounce

3 tablespoons (jigger) = 1 ½ ounces

¼ cup = 2 ounces

⅓ cup = 3 ounces

½ cup = 4 ounces

⅔ cup = 5 ounces

¾ cup = 6 ounces

1 cup = 8 ounces

1 pint = 16 ounces

1 quart = 32 ounces

750 ml bottle = 25.4 ounces

1 liter bottle = 33.8 ounces

1 medium lemon = 3 tablespoons juice

1 medium lime = 2 tablespoons juice

1 medium orange = ⅓ cup juice

Resources

FOR FURTHER READING ON ABSINTHE

WEB feeverte.net; oxygenee.com; thujone.info; wormwoodsociety.org

BOOKS *Absinthe: History in a Bottle*, by Bartleby Conrad (Chronicle Books); *Absinthe, Sip of Seduction*, by Bettina Wittels and Robert Hermesch (Speck Press)

FOR FURTHER READING ON ABSINTHE COCKTAILS AND OTHER CLASSIC COCKTAILS:

WEB cocktailchronicles.com; cocktaildb.com; imbibemagazine.com

BOOKS *The Art of the Bar*, by Jeff Hollinger and Rob Schwartz (Chronicle Books); *Imbibe! From Absinthe Cocktail to Whiskey Smash*, by David Wondrich (Perigee Trade); *Jigger, Beaker, and Glass: Drinking Around the World*, by Charles H. Baker (Derrydale Press); *Vintage Spirits and Forgotten Cocktails*, by Ted Haigh (Quarry); *The Savoy Cocktail Book*, by Harry Craddock Jr. (Pavilion)

TO PURCHASE EUROPEAN ABSINTHE THAT'S NOT AVAILABLE IN U.S. SHOPS:

absintheonline.com; feeverte.net; oxygenee.com

Index